American Board of Commissioners for Foreign Missions.

CAN THE BOARD BE KEPT OUT OF DEBT AND IN WHAT MANNER?

Sent to Pastors, and to be furnished for Gratuitous Distribution.

BOSTON:
PUBLISHED BY THE BOARD,
Missionary House, 33 Pemberton Square.
1859.

American Board of Commissioners for Foreign Missions.

CAN THE BOARD BE KEPT OUT OF DEBT, AND IN WHAT MANNER?

Sent to Pastors, and to be furnished for Gratuitous Distribution.

BOSTON:
PUBLISHED BY THE BOARD,
Missionary House, 33 Pemberton Square.
1859.

THE Prudential Committee, as instructed by the Board, send a copy of this Tract to the Pastor of every church from which donations are believed to come for the missions under their care; and they will take the liberty, also, of sending a printed statement of facts, as soon as it can be prepared, designed to aid in the preparation of a Missionary Sermon, should the Pastor be disposed (as it is earnestly hoped he may be) to preach such a sermon to his people.

The Board now enters its *Fiftieth Year*—its JUBILEE. But few now on the stage of life will live to see the *Centennial Jubilee*, in the year 1910. How affecting is it, that almost two whole generations of heathens have gone into the eternal world since the Board began its career. Should the nearly four thousand churches, with which the Board stands in connection, inheriting the blood and faith of the Puritans, now faint and grow weary under an expenditure of less than half a million of dollars, how must it chill the ardor of our expectations as to the progress and results of the work in the next fifty years! How important, then, that the Board be enabled to enter upon its new semi-centenary free of all embarrassment, and with a general and permanent rise in the contributions.

It is found, that the outlay for the year 1860 cannot be reduced below $370,000, without the *destructive* curtailments so earnestly deprecated in the following discussion. It may be important to say, that the expense of collecting the sum expended by the Board, is less than six and one-half per cent on the whole amount; and that the expense of administration is only five and one-half per cent; both of which rates, though small, will of course decrease with the growth of liberality in the churches and of the system. The remaining expenditure is directly for the missions. Now add the debt of $66,000 to the $370,000 of appropriations, and the sum needed, before the 31st of July 1860, in order to give the great enterprise a fair start for the Centenary in 1910, will be $436,000. But as the sum of the estimates sent home by the missions, of their necessary expenditures in the year 1860, called foı an expenditure of $383,000 in that year, and as the $370,000 was reached only by a pretty rough process of *economizing*, generous minds will doubtless think it better to aim at $450,000, as the sum to be raised in the Jubilee Year.

Several English Missionary Societies commenced their operations prior to the Board, and have already had their fiftieth anniversary. And they were greatly aided and stimulated in their work by the following remarkable *extra-contributions* in their year of Jubilee, without abatement in their ordinary receipts, but rather with a permanent rise in their annual incomes; viz.

The Baptist Missionary Society, in 1843, $162,500.
The London Missionary Society, in 1844, $107,500.
The Church Missionary Society, in 1849, $265,635.

We should avoid, if possible, any special appeal for liquidating the debt. How much better that the rate of the contributions be so increased, as to cover the whole needful expenditure. It should be remembered, however, that the present credit of the Board in the commercial world is of incalculable value to the churches, and will be put to some hazard by a long continuance of such an amount of indebtedness. Should the increase of the ordinary receipts not cover it, are there not enough large-hearted friends in the community to see to its extinguishment before the close of the Jubilee Year?

Missionary House, Boston, Oct. 31, 1859.

CAN THE BOARD BE KEPT OUT OF DEBT, AND IN WHAT MANNER?

I.

THE SUBJECT VIEWED FROM THE STAND-POINT OF THE MISSIONS.

This was a special report, by direction of the Prudential Committee, read by Dr. Anderson at the meeting of the Board at Philadelphia, in October, 1859. The Board, deeming the subject to be one of great importance and satisfactorily discussed, ordered the report to be printed as a tract, and sent to the pastor of every church which contributes to the funds at its disposal. It has, therefore, been put into the series of Missionary Tracts published by the Board, and pastors and others will be gratuitously furnished with as many copies as they wish for circulation.

It is time to have a better understanding as to how far it is possible, in prosecuting our Foreign Missions, to close each year without a debt. To promote such an understanding, we will discuss the subject briefly, taking our stand-point among the missions, and leaving the whole method of raising the funds for others to discuss, should there be occasion. Our effort shall be to state the law of missionary expenditure.

Though the Board has been obliged to report a debt, greater or less in amount, in thirty out of the forty-nine years of its existence, this is not because its annual expenditure has exceeded its income in so many instances. Its expenditure was really less than its income in more than half the years. But when a debt is once incurred in a great system of operations, where the demand on the treasury is constant, urgent, and increasing, it is not very easily removed; because there must be a sum large enough to pay both the current expenses and the debt. Should the expenditure of any year, for instance, be twelve thousand dollars less than the receipts, yet if the debt, at the opening of the year, be fifteen thousand dollars, there will still be a balance of three thousand against the treasury.

It is matter for grateful acknowledgment that, from the beginning to this day, there has been, on the whole, an upward tendency in the receipts. Dividing the time of the Board's existence into periods of four years, in every one of these periods, with but a single exception, there has been an increase of receipts. That single exception, it may be worth while to say, was owing to the extraordinary impression made on the Christian community by the meeting of the Board in Philadelphia, in the year 1841, which, through the divine blessing, carried the income of the following year up to the then unprecedented amount of three hundred and eighteen thousand dollars.

The difficulty all along has been, that the growth of the missions, and their increasing cost as the result of growth has been *annual* and *constant*, while it has not been so with the receipts; which have often failed for a year or more, and now for a series of years, to keep pace with the natural growth of the missions.

There are sincere friends of the cause who believe the Board ought always to be free from debt. The Prudential Committee desire this as earnestly as it is possible for any one to do, and would gladly know how such a result is to be attained. Though the duty has often been enjoined upon them, they have never yet received a practicable solution of the difficulty involved in its performance.

It is obviously impossible for a steadily increasing expenditure to be exactly met by an income subject to great annual variations. The true question, therefore, is, Shall the expenses of the missions be brought, by an inexorable process, annually repeated, to conform to the income of the Board, whatever that income may happen to be?

We shall state some of the difficulties in the way of this, on the score both of *expediency* and *possibility;* but must first describe the present usage of the Board, in making out the annual appropriations.

Previous to the great commercial crisis in the year 1837, the missions had not been placed under any positive restrictions, as to the amount of expenditure beyond which they were not at liberty to go. Just about that time commenced the great religious awakening at the Sandwich Islands, and there, and elsewhere, a tendency to enlarged expenditure began to be distinctly perceived. Consequently, that crisis found the Board in some anxious uncertainty as to the actual amount of its liabilities. This led to the adoption of the present system of *Estimates* and *Appropriations.* The missions are expected, in the course of each year, to make out a carefully prepared estimate of the expenditures needed for the next year, in every department of their labors, going as much as possible into detail, and to forward their estimate in time to reach the Missionary House before the month of October; and upon these Estimates, the Appropriations for the following year have been made out by the Prudential Committee. The missions are expected not to go beyond the appropriations.

Such is the present method of proceeding in making the annual appropriations to the several missions.

Is there another, wiser, safer, more economical plan? Shall the missions be told that, whatever the estimates and the appropriations, if the receipts shall happen to fall short, in the progress of the year, the deficiency shall be at once assessed upon them, in the form of reduced remittances? That will indeed enable the Treasurer to avoid reporting a debt; but then it will only be by virtually transferring the debt from the treasury to the several missions, to be borne and liquidated by them as best it may be. Shall new rules be laid down for governing the missions in their estimates, in order to avoid incurring a debt? They now are instructed to ask for only what they really and urgently need, for their own support, for their native helpers, for their schools, and to enable them to preach the gospel through their respective districts. Shall they be told to ask for less?

But the subject can be better discussed under the question, What is *possible?* The Board is not situated like the head of a family, with the objects of his expenditure just around him; nor like a Bible, Tract, Education, or Home Missionary Society. Its missions are beyond the sea. Its missionaries are afar off, in barbarous regions, depending for shelter, clothing, and food, wholly upon its treasury. Then, if we withdraw support from the native helpers and Christian schools, they of course all disappear; and the consequent loss of native confidence in the stability of the mission operating among them, will almost be, to their moral perceptions, like blotting the sun out of the heavens. You lose not merely the helpers, the pupils, the future stay and hope of the enterprise, but you also lose a most valuable *prestige;* you suffer a vast abatement and loss of moral power; and the missionary feels almost like a wounded soldier, stricken down on the battle field. This method of avoiding debt, if carried far and often repeated, will be mortally destructive; and therefore it is, in the strongest sense, impossible.

Take, for illustration, the estimates and appropriations for the coming year. The appropriations are not yet made; but the whole amount of these estimates is $380,000. Should we cut them down $30,000, so as to allow an expenditure of only $350,000, even then it will require an income of $416,000 to enable the Board to assemble free of debt at its fiftieth anniversary. How shall the Committee, with this reduction, arrange the appropriations for the missions? They are, it is supposed, to reduce the sum of the estimates $30,000. In cutting off sources of expense, some regard must of course be had to the relative value of each department of expense; though, in point of fact, the reduction will never be levied wholly upon one, or even two, of the departments. The order of valuation is something like this: 1. The missionaries; 2. Native pastors; 3. Native preachers; 4. Catechists; 5. The higher training schools for helpers; and 6. The common schools. Then there is the press, standing intimately related to all these. Some regard must be had to this scale of valuation. Were a clean sweep to be made of the common schools, even that would not save so much as two thirds of the sum; and were the residue to be assessed upon the higher schools, what a wave of desolation would there be in this method of relieving the charities of the churches! Or were the whole assessed on the native pastors, preachers, and helpers, some four or five hundred in number, that would deprive the missions of nearly the entire body; whose education must have cost at least one hundred and fifty thousand dollars, besides years of anxious labor and care. Is such a reduction to be regarded as *possible?* Let him who so believes, go to the Committee Room, some time in the present month, and try his own skill at destroying the fruits of missionary self-denial and toil, the answers to so many prayers.

The gradual increase in the receipts of the Board, prior to the year 1853, sufficed, on the whole, to meet the growth of the missions until that time; but it has not been so in the last six years. This is owing to the more rapid increase in the growth and consequent cost of the missions; mainly to the greater success of our work, and the more abundant answers to our prayers. It is not the result, however, of an increase in the number of ordained missionaries; for that is only eight more the present year than it was six years ago, and but ten more than it was ten years ago. Indeed, the Board sent thirty more missionaries in the ten years preceding its meeting in Philadelphia eighteen years ago, than it did in the ten years last past. Yet in the last ten years the heathen world has been providentially opening with wonderful rapidity, bringing scores of millions, and even hundreds of millions, within reach of the Gospel; and the churches have been apprised of this fact. The new missionaries do but little more than supply the waste from sickness and death. Therefore we should pray, not only for increased funds, but even with greater earnestness, that the Lord of the harvest will send forth laborers into his harvest. There is no danger in sending forth suitable missionaries. Every such missionary may be regarded as insuring, on the whole, his own support, by a reacting influence upon the churches. The practical difficulty is in securing the means of sustaining what may be called the *auxiliary* forces — the native helpers, schools, printing, etc. These, in some of the more advanced and prosperous missions, cost considerably more than the missionaries themselves, sometimes not less than twice as much. Yet the native converts, churches, pastors, preachers, teachers, schools, are just what, through the divine blessing, we are seeking to create. Without them we labor in vain. They are the beginning of Christian churches and Christian communities; and it is of no use to send the missionaries, if we do not support and cherish these.

The result we come to is this: That we must provide for the *growth* and *development* of the tree, as well as for *planting* it; for gathering and preserving the harvest, as well as for sowing the seed. It is true, that the expenditure of the missions needs always to be carefully guarded, and sometimes curtailed. There are great economical questions in the conduct of missions. But curtailments which *destroy* the fruits of missionary labor are always a calamity. They are to be treated as calamities. They will fail us as a preventive of debt. One such is sure to prepare the way for another, and that for another. They encourage, they animate, no one. They never open, they close, the heart of benevolence. They are a retreat in the presence of an enemy, to be attempted only when there is no other escape from greater disasters.

Yet if it be really a fact that our sphere is too broad for our ability, it would be better to reduce the *number* of the missions, than often to subject them to disastrous curtailments. Suppose, then, that we undertake to relieve the overburdened churches in this way. Where the discontinued mission is not merely an attempt at concentration of effort in some of the larger fields — which is sometimes good economy — this will not be found so very easy a matter. Suppose, for instance, that we resolve to retire from Western Africa. It will cost us as many thousands, the first year, to bring the missionaries home, and support them till they can support themselves, as it does now. And then the *lamentations!* — of the missionaries, and of the tens of thousands who feel, and pray, and labor for Africa and her oppressed sons! Suppose we retire from Micronesia. We then hazard a serious spiritual loss at the Sandwich Islands, where both missionaries and people need the reacting influence of this *to them* foreign mission. Indeed we shall discover, that a withdrawal from any considerable field, already occupied, and long enough in existence to create an interest at home, will more or less weaken the hold of the general cause upon the churches, and the influence of our appeals. And it is, besides, a serious question for us to consider, whether our present system of missions has really *a greater variety* of peoples and languages than is needful for its convenient and efficient working. For it will be found easier to obtain support for a large and varied system of missions, than for a small one with poverty of detail and feebleness of impression.

Our *first* answer, therefore, to the question proposed at the outset, is: That the Board can not expect to keep out of debt by means of such curtailments as are positively *destructive*.

Our *second* is: That the Board can keep out of debt only by observing the *law of continued growth*, which God has prescribed for the missionary enterprise. We can have healthy, contented, prosperous missions, only so long as we secure for them a free growth and expansion. And it has ever been the policy of the Board, having regard to this law, to protect, as far as possible, the results of labor in the missions. It is this which has kept the expenditure generally in advance, somewhat, of the public sentiment, as expressed in the contributions.

Our *third* and last answer is: That the Board can be kept out of debt only by a growth in the contributions *corresponding* to the natural growth in the missions. Better not begin a mission, than afterwards to fail of sustaining it. And whenever a mission is spiritually quickened, and thus accelerated in its growth, then, for a longer or shorter course of years, there will be a demand for increase in the outlay and contributions. To require *prosperous* missions, while the means for their healthful growth are withheld, is somewhat like Pharaoh's requisition upon the poor Israelites, of bricks without straw.

This whole subject is confessedly one of great practical difficulty, and needs a more thorough consideration than it has yet received by the community. While we once more avow as strong a repugnance, on the part of the Prudential Committee, to an excess of expenditure, as any donor can feel, we maintain the impossibility, with a large and prosperous system of distant missions, of making the treasury always free and joyous at the year's end, if there be an uncertain and greatly varying income.

In conclusion, facts would seem to indicate that the Lord addresses us in the Prophet's language of expostulation to the ancient Church: "If thou hast run with the footmen, and they have wearied thee, then how canst thou contend with horses? And if in the land of peace, wherein thou trustedst, they wearied thee, then how wilt thou do in the swelling of Jordan?"

II.

THE SUBJECT VIEWED FROM AN AMERICAN STAND-POINT.

After the foregoing special report had been read to the Board, Dr. Pomroy, the Secretary having charge of the Home Department, addressed the Board in a speech, which was substantially as follows: —

He said he would look at the condition of the treasury for a moment from an American stand-point. Dr. Anderson had told us how the subject presents itself when viewed from the foreign field; he (Dr. P.) would look at it from this platform, here in Philadelphia.

As a Board, and as a Christian community, we have now reached a point in the progress of Foreign Missions, where it is proper to pause and take a survey of the past. We have entered on our fiftieth year — the Year of Jubilee. Let us call to mind the way in which the Lord has led us; considering the manifold interpositions of his gracious providence, the wonderful outpourings of his Spirit in different parts of the great field; dropping a tear over the graves of those noble men and women who have fallen in the conflict, and lie buried on distant continents and islands of the sea; and looking not merely at the past, but also at the present and the future. The occasion is a great one, a noble one; let us turn it to the best account, and make our doings worthy of it.

Look out, now, and see what God has been and is doing, in the dark places of the earth. The Turkish Empire is open; the crescent is protecting the cross; the Gospel is having free course, and exerting a power in those ancient lands unsurpassed since the days of Paul. India is opening her broad and inviting fields to the reaper, and old England will soon see that there shall be no ban upon the Word of God there. The brazen gates of China and Japan are breaking, falling, and all the millions of their benighted people will soon be accessible to the Christian missionary. The islands of the Pacific are waiting and calling for the Gospel. The veil has been lifted from the dark regions of Africa. Papal Europe is trembling to its centre. The Pope retains his seat in Rome by the sufferance of one man in Paris. The empire of the Sultan exists because Christian Europe has said, Let it alone for the present. Within the last five years, numerous and mighty barriers to the progress of the Gospel have been demolished, one after another, in various parts of the earth; filling the nations with wonder at that which has come to pass, and calling upon the Christians of this and other lands to go forth, and publish the everlasting Gospel to the people who sit in the region and shadow of death. It would seem as if the time had come, when the nation and kingdom that undertakes to exclude the Gospel from its limits is to be "dashed in pieces." Never, in the whole history of Christianity, as it seems to me, have the movements of divine Providence been so marvelous as within the last few years. Never was the great field so accessible, so inviting, at almost all points.

Look at our own country. Within the last two years converts have been gathered into the fold of Christ by hundreds of thousands, many of them in the morning of life. When and where, since the apostolic age, have such blessed scenes been witnessed? What meaneth this? Is not God saying to his people, most emphatically, "Go forward"? The Red Sea is rolling back its waves; Jordan is standing "on heaps"; Canaan is in full view. What shall we do? Shall we turn back? Shall we stand still? Or shall we go in and take possession in the name of the Great King? And yet here we are, at this great meeting, in the city of Philadelphia — with all our resources, all our commerce, all our wealth, all our opening prospects — perplexed, troubled, anxious, about what? SOME SIXTY OR SEVENTY THOUSAND DOLLARS! And yet there are individual Christian merchants, here in Philadelphia, in New York, in Boston, and other cities, who could wipe off that debt in five minutes, without the slightest embarrassment to their business. If it were a promising scheme for speculation, you might go over to Chestnut Street, near by, and secure a hundred thousand dollars in less than an hour. As Christian men and women, we ought to get down upon our knees, and sue for mercy.

The DEBT! Some people think that the Prudential Committee at Boston like to be in debt. But I tell you, there is not a man at the Missionary House on Pemberton Square who does not dislike a debt quite as much as any one here. We try to avoid it. We give our entire assent to the document which has just been read by Dr. Anderson. But when you say, Take the knife and cut down the missions, send away the native pastors, scatter the little churches, break up the schools, and send the children back into the jaws of heathenism — we pause; we are not quite ready for that. We are not quite sure that either God or his people wish us to do such a deed as that. We incline to think it neither wise nor expedient to make a great ado about this debt; but rather let proclamation be made, that the Lord Jesus Christ the Great Missionary from heaven, wants this year an advance of AT LEAST ONE HUNDRED THOUSAND DOLLARS in the receipts of the Board. This could be made, and not a man of us lose a dinner or a supper.

The speaker would beg leave to suggest two or three things in regard to this Year of Jubilee, on which we are entering. In the first place; let every pastor, whose congregation sustains this Board, prepare and preach, perhaps on a stated day, to be suggested by the Prudential Committee, a sermon — an historical, eloquent, powerful sermon, surveying the whole field. I say eloquent — for no one can throw himself into such a theme and not be eloquent. It will carry him even beyond himself. Let every pastor, therefore, blow the trumpet which God has put in his hand. If it be a golden one, all the better — blow that; if silver, blow that; if it chance to be a brazen bugle, blow that; and if it be nothing better than a ram's horn, still let him blow it, and remember Jericho. It will do him good, and his people good, and the world good; and though he may not know it, its influence will be felt in distant regions, and onward through coming ages, long after he shall have moldered back to dust. It may be desirable that this should be done *on the same Sabbath by all.*

In the next place; when this sermon shall be preached, let arrangements be made for a glorious JUBILEE COLLECTION; not with reference to any specific thing, such as paying off the debt — but a jubilee collection that will make all hearts glad; one that will tell on the old world, and make that glad; on the heathen, and make them glad; on the toilworn missionary, and make him glad; — a collection that will push on the missionary enterprise in a manner never yet equaled.* Now, in this year of jubilee, is the time to "change the switch," and go on to the conquest of the world. Why should not contributors *double* their subscription, or contribution? And let those professed followers of Christ who seldom or never do any thing for this cause, *begin to do their duty,* and make amends for past neglect. Surely the pastors, and churches, and people of these United States, whom God has so greatly blessed, will see that this thing is done — and done in a way that will redound to the glory of Him in whom is all their hope and all their salvation. Let every man, woman, and child have a hand in this

* This was in the speech, as delivered before the Board. The most effectual manner of securing the desired increase in the contributions of the year, can best be determined by those on the ground — pastors and people.

blessed enterprise. If any need encouragements, let them look at the past. The Board began small. It was doubtful, at the first, whether the churches of this country could sustain the three or four young men who offered themselves. One of them was sent to old England, to see if the London Missionary Society would come to our aid, in case we should fail in such a mighty enterprise as that of supporting three or four young men on heathen shores. That noble society said, "Go forward; we will stand by you, and help you, if necessary." Now we have one hundred and seventy ordained missionaries, and a little less than one thousand laborers in the field, of all descriptions. Why should we doubt, or falter? The sun never sets on the missions of this Board; and what is infinitely more and better, the Sun of Righteousness has never ceased to shine upon them, from the first day until now.

Another encouragement is found in the fact that millions of benighted people are calling to us for the gospel. A few years since, a letter came to Boston from the Feegee Islands, in the South Pacific Ocean, brought by the captain of a whale ship, signed by several chiefs, each making his mark. The substance of it was: "We have heard what you have done for the Sandwich Islands; we also want missionaries; will you not send them to us?" We could not send them, but the English Wesleyans sent missionaries there; and a few weeks since, Mr. Arthur, one of the secretaries of that society, told me there was no more interesting missionary field in the world than those Feegee Islands. God awakened the desire in their hearts for teachers, and when the Gospel reached them, they said, "This is what we wanted." It is just so at this moment in Africa, Western Asia, India, China, and many other countries.

And now for the grand motive to missionary effort — what is it? *The love of Christ.* This is the mightiest power that ever moved upon the soul of man. Did you ever feel it? It can take a man to any part of the world, carry him through all toils, and sacrifices, and sufferings, even to a martyr's grave; and when he has done all, and suffered all, he will feel that he has done nothing in comparison with what Christ has done for him. If the love of Christ is in our hearts, it *must*, it WILL show itself in personal sacrifices for him and his cause. Dear brethren and friends, will you not give your hearts and hands to this great and blessed work? In heaven it will be sweet to think that we did something for Him who has done so much for us.

III.

THE RESPONSE OF THE BOARD.

The case, thus presented, was referred by the Board to a Committee, composed of Dr. Child, Dr. Duffield, Chancellor Walworth, Dr. Todd, Rev. H. G. Ludlow, A. W. Porter, Esq., and N. Durfee, M. D., who subsequently made the following report, which was adopted: —

The Committee on the Domestic Department, and upon the Special Report of the Prudential Committee concerning the question, "Can the Board be kept out of debt, and in what manner?" would report: That they have carefully examined the papers committed to them, and are impressed with the consideration, that the present condition of the missionary operations of the Board imperatively demands, that the churches which have constituted this Board their almoners, should come to a better understanding of the nature, methods, and results of the great work in which they are engaged. The Committee are unanimously and fully of the opinion, that the present debt of the Board, in the circumstances of the case, could not have been avoided by the Prudential Committee, without incurring evils compared with which such a debt is an inconsiderable trifle. The debt is wholly the result of the prosperity of the work for which missions are undertaken; this prosperity involving the necessity for increased expenditure, and this increased expenditure not being provided for by the contributions of the churches, on which all depended. This subject is presented in a clear, convincing light, in the paper submitted to the Board. And this paper is not merely explanatory of the fact of the present indebtedness of the Board, but discloses also a law which pertains to all successful missionary operations. Their very success must involve the necessity of increased expenditure, unless you would start back from the work you have undertaken, and sacrifice all you have gained. It is a question, then, for the churches to consider and determine, whether they will go on in the work they have commenced, and conform to the requirement which the prosperity with which God blesses them involves. Did they not enter upon it because they believed that the command of their Redeemer required it at their hands? And is he not owning their work, and fulfilling toward them his own assurance, "Lo, I am with you"? Under such circumstances, can they do otherwise than go forward? And is there really a heavier burden upon the churches now, in proportion to their ability to meet the exigencies of the case, than there was when they began? Have not the resources of the church been increased in a far greater ratio than the demands made upon them by the state of missionary operations? Where are the tens of thousands who have entered the churches in the recent great revivals; and where the increasing wealth of those who have professed to give themselves, and their possessions, and all their means of influence, to Him who has redeemed them with his own blood? It can not be doubted that the ability of the churches is fully adequate to the work which imperatively calls them, and the performance of which will be as full of blessings to themselves as to the objects of their benevolence. Your committee are fully persuaded, that if this subject should be duly brought home to the understanding, conscience, and heart of the friends of Christ who are patrons of the Board, they would pray the Board, with great importunity, not only to abstain from any such retrenchment as would seriously impede the prosperity with which God is favoring them, but to follow any plain, divine leadings for enlargement. As means of placing this matter before the churches in its true light, and effecting that conviction which their duty and their best interests alike demand, your committee would recommend, —

1. That this Special Report be published as a tract, and a copy sent to every pastor of the churches who would patronize the operations of this Board.

2. That such pastors be earnestly requested to preach, at least once in every year, directly and fully, upon the duty resting upon all who have received the gospel to do what they can to fulfill the last command of Christ: "Go ye into all the world, and preach the Gospel to every creature." And, —

3. As we are now entering upon the Year of Jubilee, that Christians be encouraged to make their offerings worthy of the good hand of God upon them, and of such an era in the history of their missionary efforts, by a marked increase in the amount of their individual contributions; regarding such an increase as a pledge of their intention, relying upon the grace and blessing of their Lord to adopt, henceforward, a higher standard of missionary zeal and benevolence.

We recommend that the Prudential Committee be left at full liberty — if in the course of the year they shall find it necessary — to use any special means to effect the objects now contemplated, which their wisdom may devise.

Let it be understood, that the accomplishment of what is needed in this crisis will depend very much upon the fidelity of the ministers of Christ, as the instructors and guides of his people. If they shall get their own minds fully impressed with the obligations of this great work, and their souls inspired with all the grand and commanding motives which persuade to its performance, they will be eloquent; and we hazard nothing in saying, they will be greatly successful. Ought they not to feel that they are "brought to the kingdom for such a time as this"? Ought they not to be discerners of this time, when the providences of God, and the dispensations of his grace, seem to be loudly calling upon the church to give the world the knowledge of her Redeemer? And if they shall fail in their duty, does it not seem likely that enlargement and deliverance will arise from some other quarter, while they and their fathers' house shall come to poverty? We do not mean to lay any heavier burdens upon the ministry than those which their Lord imposes. We believe that, so far as the giving of money is concerned, they have, as a body, given more than any other equal number of men, in proportion to their ability. It is as the teachers and guides of the Lord's people that we speak of them, and of their obligation to do what they can to set forth to the churches the facts, and principles, and motives which are urging them to hasten, by all the means in their power, the conversion of the world to Christ. And we are fully persuaded, that there is no way in which the Christian pastor can more effectually labor to teach the members of his church to give all diligence to the full assurance of their own hope of eternal life, than by leading them to a devotion of all their powers, and means of influence, to the glory of their Redeemer, in the salvation of the world for which he died.

www.ingramcontent.com/pod-product-compliance
Lightning Source LLC
LaVergne TN
LVHW011140110826
845150LV00008B/2439

* 9 7 8 1 4 1 8 1 9 3 4 4 7 *